Color & Sleuth
HAUNTED CITY
A Spooky Coloring Mystery

Rebecca Demos

with Ellie Alexander

Quarto.com | WalterFoster.com

© 2025 Quarto Publishing Group USA Inc.
Text and Illustrations © 2025 Rebecca Demos

First Published in 2025 by Walter Foster Publishing, an imprint of The Quarto Group, 100 Cummings Center, Suite 265-D, Beverly, MA 01915, USA.
T (978) 282-9590 F (978) 283-2742

All rights reserved. No part of this book may be reproduced in any form without written permission of the copyright owners. All images in this book have been reproduced with the knowledge and prior consent of the artists concerned, and no responsibility is accepted by producer, publisher, or printer for any infringement of copyright or otherwise, arising from the contents of this publication. Every effort has been made to ensure that credits accurately comply with information supplied. We apologize for any inaccuracies that may have occurred and will resolve inaccurate or missing information in a subsequent reprinting of the book.

Walter Foster Publishing titles are also available at discount for retail, wholesale, promotional, and bulk purchase. For details, contact the Special Sales Manager by email at specialsales@quarto.com or by mail at The Quarto Group, Attn: Special Sales Manager, 100 Cummings Center, Suite 265-D, Beverly, MA 01915, USA.

29 28 27 26 25   2 3 4 5

ISBN: 978-0-7603-9772-5

Digital edition published in 2025
eISBN: 978-0-7603-9773-2

Design: Rebecca Demos and *tabula rasa* graphic design
Page Layout: *tabula rasa* graphic design

Printed in China

Acknowledgments

A heartfelt thank-you to Michelle Bredeson from Quarto—truly the best acquisitions editor on the planet. Your guidance and vision have been invaluable. To Ellie Alexander, whose incredible skill and craft brought this project to life, I'm endlessly grateful. And to my husband, Chris—you are the best part of me. Your unwavering support and love make everything possible. Like, isn't this crazy? —R. D.

I'm deeply grateful to have been part of this project. Thank you so much to Michelle Bredeson for your guidance on the story and vision and to the team at Quarto for bringing this project into the world. Rebecca Demos, it's been an utter delight to collaborate with you! Thank you for the opportunity to bring a little snark to this whimsical, cozy world. I can't wait to curl up with these sneaky ghosts and break out my colored pencils. —E. A.

INTRODUCING

Color & Sleuth Spooky Coloring Mysteries

The **Color & Sleuth** series is a brand-new concept in coloring—and puzzle books! **Color & Sleuth** invites you into a whimsical world where adorable ghosts dwell in spooky houses, haunted apartment buildings, and sinister farms and take ghostly getaways. Each page is a canvas for both coloring and sleuthing and is accompanied by a scene from the story that includes clues to unravel a mystery. By the end, you will use the clues you have gathered from the images and the text to answer four questions and solve the mystery. Get them right, and you will be awarded with downloadable prizes.

Listen & Sleuth
Use this QR code to access a specially curated playlist. It will help put you in a spooky mood as you color and sleuth.

HOW IT WORKS

1 Get the scoop from the resident gossip columnist about all the strange happenings at the Pigeon Court Apartments.

Pigeon Hallows Daily
The Court Report

Green Isn't Your Color

Could it be that Dorothea has a touch of envy? She can't be bothered with Eleanor. She has her own commissioned pieces to finish. Now, if she can only convince Clarence to buy one of her necklaces to replace the missing jewel. Is "convince" the word I'm looking for or is "blackmail" a bit more appropriate? Dorothea is pinning her hopes on her new green glass beads. Can they give her jewelry store a much-needed boost in sales? It's anyone's guess at this point.

—Forever lurking
xxxx

2 Search for more clues while you color.

Notes:

SUSPECTS

Print extra note pages by scanning the QR code.

CLUES

NOTES

3 Keep track of suspects and clues on the note pages at the back of the book.

4 Answer four questions to solve the mystery!

In Color & Sleuth: HAUNTED CITY

you will use your deduction and reasoning skills to answer these four questions and solve the mystery:

Who stole the jewel?

Who broke the elevator?

Who is stealing packages?

Whose bones are in the basement?

OUR STORY BEGINS...

Welcome to Pigeon Court!

The residents of this five-story apartment building seem so nice and friendly—but dark secrets lurk behind their doors. They'd love your help solving some mysteries that have been occurring there lately. Are you brave enough to come inside?

Pigeon Hallows Daily

Darkmoor Family Jewel Stolen!

$13,000 reward for any information about the missing jewel—last seen at the Darkmoor residence at the Pigeon Court Apartments by Clarence Darkmoor.

Pigeon Court Apartments

The Court Report

Court is in session, and I require your assistance. As your humble gossip columnist, I shall commit to bringing you news of the strange happenings in our beloved building. Come on a journey through our hallowed hallways. You'll meet an eclectic group of resident ghosts (some of whom are up to no good). The question is, who is causing such chaos? The clues are piling up, and time is of the essence. Make haste and proceed with caution.

—Forever lurking xxxx

Welcome, dearest departed.

Percival is available to assist with your every need. Excepting umbrellas, of course. They keep wandering off. This is why we can't have nice things.

Don't leave packages unattended!

Collect mail promptly—packages gone missing. Elevator under repair. Use stairs.

Will be fixed soon.

Percy

Pigeon Hallows Daily
The Court Report

I wish I could rest in peace in this afterlife, but someone has to keep this community on the straight and narrow, and I suppose it will have to be me—the sacrifices I make for you. Sigh. Shall we start with Rhett? He's been caught napping on one too many occasions. In my humble opinion, the source of his sleepiness can only be explained by his recent cohabitation. He had better adjust quickly. His weekly club meeting is tonight, and he can't be caught dozing off again. Time for a shot of espresso, perhaps?

—Forever lurking

xxxx

Pigeon Hallows Daily
The Court Report

Have you heard love songs wafting through the corridors? My sources say the music is coming from Rhett's apartment. His now live-in girlfriend, who shall remain nameless, has a penchant for romantic ballads. Rumor has it that her coveted apartment is vacant. Ooohhh, this means new neighbors and juicy new gossip coming soon. Stay tuned, my lovely ghosts and ghouls.

—Forever lurking

xxxx

Pigeon Hallows Daily
The Court Report

Through the grapevine, I've learned that Eleanor's latest art installation is progressing nicely, but it's missing a key element—bowling balls. Yes, you read that correctly. Don't ask me. She's the *artiste*. I'm on pins and needles waiting to see how it will come together. Speaking of pins, Harold seems to have commandeered her extra bowling balls. Why? Has he taken up the sport? You know, he was banned from the garden club. My lips are sealed, but I'm glad he's looking for a new pastime.

—Forever lurking

xxxx

Pigeon Hallows Daily
The Court Report

Well, Dorothea isn't playing, is she? She deserves an Oscar for her acting performance. Yours truly spotted her breezing past the yellow flier tacked to her door as if she'd never seen it. Have you had enough of Eleanor's art, or are you just dying for a shower, Dorothea? My bet is on the latter.

—Forever lurking

✗✗✗✗

Pigeon Hallows Daily

The Court Report

Green Isn't Your Color

Could it be that Dorothea has a touch of envy? She can't be bothered with Eleanor. She has her own commissioned pieces to finish. Now, if she can only convince Clarence to buy one of her necklaces to replace the missing jewel. Is "convince" the word I'm looking for, or is "blackmail" a bit more appropriate? Dorothea is pinning her hopes on her new green glass beads. Can they give her jewelry store a much-needed boost in sales? It's anyone's guess at this point.

—Forever lurking

xxxx

Pigeon Hallows Daily
The Court Report

Dorothea has a little secret up her sleeve. How is her jewelry so superior and sturdy, you might ask? Fear not. I have the answer, as always. Wait for it . . . Dorothea sources her string from her brother's old fishing rod. Thrifty and sustainable. Clever, clever.

—Forever lurking

xxxx

Pigeon Hallows Daily
The Court Report

All that fine detail work seems to have tuckered Dorothea out. My suggestion? Indulge in a steaming hot bubble bath and admire your pretty pink tile before the water runs out in your unit, too. Don't forget your manners, though. I have it on good authority that you owe Richport a thank-you note. You can drop it off on your way to pick up Polly at your brother's. Have a good soak, but don't forget your neighborly duties. Remember, a simple thank-you goes a long way.

—Forever lurking

xxxx

Pigeon Hallows Daily

The Court Report

Gwendolyn is sulking. Not a good look, darling. Although, in fairness, nothing seems to be going right. Her festive green and black flags keep falling, and her daughter is less than impressed with her attempts to brighten the dreary hallway. Don't be dismayed, Gwennie. Can I call you Gwennie? Your yellow string lights are a beacon of delight. I, for one, wholeheartedly approve of bringing some cheer to the Pigeon Court drear.

—Forever lurking

xxxx

Pigeon Hallows Daily
The Court Report

Here's a sneaky bit of news: Gwendolyn has called in reinforcements—the one and only Polly. As those of us "in the know" understand, Polly is a bit of a prodigy, a born artist, you might say. She'll make quick work of this mess. Her eagle eye doesn't miss anything, which only infuriates Eleanor. *Gwendolyn*, when did you become so diabolical? I'm enjoying this side of you.

—Forever lurking

xxxx

Pigeon Hallows Daily

The Court Report

Leroy's fern could use some love. What an unbecoming shade of brown. His cactus seems to be holding up fine in this ongoing water crisis. Gwendolyn tried to warn him that a cactus was more his style—unkillable. Perhaps he should have listened to the green thumb. But none of it matters if Elmer doesn't fix the building's pipes soon; the fern is short for this afterlife, and so are we. I don't know about you, but I'm practically parched. What I wouldn't do for a long, hot shower.

—Forever lurking

xxxx

Pigeon Hallows Daily
The Court Report

Leroy, you might want to devote some attention to your floors. Aren't you hosting guests later? Those blue footprints aren't a good look. I find a quick and easy task list helpful in situations like this. Let's check off your tasks, shall we?

- Mop
- Find missing boot
- Make an appearance at Eleanor's "art" show

Chop, chop. Time is ticking.

—Forever lurking

xxxx

Pigeon Hallows Daily

The Court Report

Have you heard? It's poker night at Leroy's. Not invited? What a shame. But don't be dismayed. There could be an empty seat as Dorothea has yet to RSVP. Could she be concerned that she'll finally be found out for her cheating? But then again, I've heard rumblings that Leroy always insists on using his pair of lucky dice. What exactly makes them "lucky," Leroy? Do tell.

—Forever lurking

xxxx

Pigeon Hallows Daily
The Court Report

Has the stress finally gotten to Leroy? The players are dropping like flies. His best friend Vernon has given up his gambling ways in favor of the finer things in life— fancy dinner parties and expensive fishing trips. Here's a little something to nibble on—how has Vernon come into funds? A good hand or two at poker or . . . well, I'll leave it there for now as I'm never one to speculate.

—Forever lurking

Pigeon Hallows Daily
The Court Report

Body shaming? That's what we've stooped to? I think not. Poor Eugene. What a travesty to arrive home after a long day only to find diet pamphlets on his door. Tasteless. Tacky. Not at all up to the standards of our beloved Pigeon Court. A word to the wise: I wouldn't underestimate Eugene. He has powerful friends with deep pockets who aren't afraid to make people disappear, as in *permanently*.

—Forever lurking

xxxx

Pigeon Hallows Daily
The Court Report

Have you poured yourself a cuppa? Good. Settle in, dear reader, because I have some serious scoop. Eugene still hasn't cleaned up Clarence's mess from the infamous dinner. Hold onto your tea cups. Here's what we know: Clarence flipped the entire table when he learned his jewel was missing. Yikes. Eugene's attempts to find the missing jewel were futile. The police were summoned, guests were questioned then cleared, and the apartment was scoured—nothing was found. The plot thickens.

—Forever lurking

xxxx

The Court Report

What is that stack of blue suitcases doing in Elmer's apartment? Not trying to make a break for it, are you, Elmer? Is he ready to run? He certainly seems skittish with all the police activity in the building. He's fooled almost everyone, but the mounting tenant complaints about the water have me suspecting there's much more to uncover about our resident handyman.

—Forever lurking
XXXX

Pigeon Hallows Daily

The Court Report

My instincts about Elmer were correct—no surprise. My sources say Percy should be shouldering some of the blame. He hired Elmer without doing his due diligence. Elmer constructed a simple birdhouse for his cousin Finch, but if Percy had dug deeper, he would have learned Elmer can't even repair the hole in his apartment wall, let alone the entire building's plumbing system or elevator. It's stairs and takeout for us indefinitely, my dears.

—Forever lurking

xxxx

Pigeon Hallows Daily
The Court Report

Things have gone from bad to worse for our super. No water. A broken elevator. And add faulty surveillance cameras to the list. After Clarence reported his jewel had been stolen, Percy dutifully reviewed the footage only to discover that two of the videos wouldn't load. Interesting, isn't it? One might also say convenient. Let's check it out for ourselves!

—Forever lurking

xxxx

Pigeon Hallows Daily
The Court Report

Harold has some thoughts, and unlike Percy, he is *not* open to suggestions. When I graciously asked him a question or two for our community report, he balked and became quite defensive. Since I am a pillar of truth and a most ardent journalist, let me repeat his words verbatim: "I did not steal the bowling ball. I merely borrowed it. I did not steal the umbrellas or packages from the lobby. It wasn't me!" Oh, Harold, I do believe the gentleman doth protest too much.

—Forever lurking

xxxx

Pigeon Hallows Daily
The Court Report

A concerned resident has informed me that underneath Harold's prickly exterior, there's a cozy, warm teddy bear. Could it be true? According to my nameless source, his heart melts in a mushy puddle whenever the love of his life is near. Where did she scurry off to? I can't say, but I do caution you not to poke the bear, just in case.

—Forever lurking

xxxx

Pigeon Hallows Daily
The Court Report

What's this? A special package of red and maroon fabrics? Harold can't believe Elmer came through on his promise to send him new designs, and quite frankly, neither can I. How fetching his darling Etta will look in them, especially with the extra embellishments Elmer added—sparkly bows and sequins. Someone's getting fancy, aren't they?

—Forever lurking

xxxx

Pigeon Hallows Daily
The Court Report

What a stunner. Elmer has absolutely outdone himself this time. The dress should grace runways and is a perfect fit for Etta. Harold will have to think of a way to repay Elmer for his luxurious designs. It's just the pick-me-up Etta needs after having her life threatened. What? You haven't heard about her near miss? Oh yes, my intel is correct on that, my dearests.

—Forever lurking

xxxx

Hallows Historical Society 1

Pigeon Hallows Daily
Court Report

Richport is up against a deadline. That's something I'm very familiar with in the biz, as we like to say. His speech for the historical society is seriously lacking in content and context. Time to crack those knuckles and pound out those words on the keyboard. Time is ticking. What's that? You're distracted by your roommate? Richie, I have news for you; that's nothing more than an excuse. And frankly, not a good one.

—Forever lurking

xxxx

Pigeon Hallows Daily
The Court Report

Like many of us, Richport was shaken up by the theft of Clarence's family jewel and being questioned by the police. After the authorities departed, he wasted no time boarding up Clarence's penthouse as if to seal off the chaos. But one nagging detail continues to plague him. A most critical observation: The jewel wasn't taken from the penthouse. So where was it stolen from, and how did the thief pull it off? Questions abound. There's more to this mystery than meets the eye.

—Forever lurking

xxxx

Pigeon Hallows Daily

The Court Report

To help ease Clarence's anxiety, Richport has retrieved the building blueprints and stumbled upon something most revealing. There's no way in or out of the penthouse except for the elevator. The only other possible way of getting into any of the apartments—other than through the front door—is via the handful of ceiling hatches. Do tell, why has the elevator been out of commission then? My dearly departed, I do believe we have a locked-room mystery on our hands.

—Forever lurking

xxxx

Pigeon Hallows Daily
The Court Report

Have you cracked the case, my clever ghostly ghoul? Well done. Bravo! Your sleuthing skills deserve special recognition. As a reward for your sharp mind, the key to the penthouse awaits—if you dare to take it.

And so, dear readers, this edition of the Court Report comes to a close. However, yours truly will remain ever-watchful, lurking in the shadows and hallways, waiting to uncover the next mystery that reveals itself.

—Forever lurking

xxxx

Have you solved the mystery, my ghouls?
Check the QR codes below to see if you've cracked the case and prepare to be rewarded with a special gift from yours truly. I couldn't have done it without you. Bravo!

Who stole the jewel?	Who broke the elevator?	Who is stealing packages?	Whose bones are in the basement?
A. Eugene	D. Elmer	G. Eleanor	J. Doris
B. Percy	E. Polly	H. Rhett	K. Dorothea
C. Vernon	F. Harold	I. Gwendolyn	L. Lidia

ADGL    ADGK    BEIL    BEIJ

CDIK    CDIJ    CEHK    BFHK

BFHJ    BFIK    AFIL    AFIJ

AFIK    BFHJ    BEGK    BEGL

Until next time . . .

When you work out the Mystery and scan the correct QR code, you will be rewarded with a downloadable coloring poster to continue your coloring adventures in Pigeon Hallows. Here's a sneak peek!

Notes:

Print extra note pages by scanning the QR code.

Clues

Notes

Rebecca Demos

Rebecca Demos is the creator of the Color & Sleuth series. A self-described board game junkie, she is obsessed with puzzles. Rebecca is the author of more than a dozen children's books and has illustrated twenty-four books for Leap for Literacy, a nonprofit that publishes books written by children. She is also an illustrator for several podcasts, including the *Generation Why* and *Once Upon a Crime* true crime podcasts. Rebecca lives with her family in Chicago.

Ellie Alexander

Ellie Alexander is the author of more than forty mystery novels, including the Bakeshop Mysteries and the Sloan Krause Mysteries. She is also a writing teacher and coach. Ellie lives with her family in Northern California.